Moon Symphony

A Symphony of Poems

Yusra Ayaz

BookLeaf Publishing

India | USA | UK

Made with ❤ on the BookLeaf Publishing Platform
www.bookleafpub.in
www.bookleafpub.com

Dedication

"To my mother, who taught me the value of persistence and love. Thank you for always pushing me to pursue my passion. This book is for you."

Preface

The poems in this collection are fragments of my own journey—pieces of love, loss, and hope stitched together over countless nights. They are as much a reflection of me as they are of the world around us.

The journey of writing this book has been one of self-discovery. These pages hold my most vulnerable truths, shaped by love, loss, and the quiet strength of resilience. They are as much yours as they are mine.

I wrote this for the dreamers, the seekers, and the ones who find solace in words. May this collection offer you comfort, connection, and perhaps a glimpse of your own story within its lines.

With Gratitude,
Yusra

Acknowledgements

No book is ever truly a solo endeavor, and this one is no exception. I owe a debt of gratitude to the many hearts and hands that helped bring this collection to life.

To my family, for their unwavering belief in me—even on the days when I doubted myself. Your love has been the bedrock of all that I create.

To my friends, who lent me their ears, their encouragement, and their unwavering faith in me. I cannot express how thankful I am to you all for listening to my late-night rants —thank you for being my anchors and my cheerleaders.

A special thanks to my editor, [Name], whose keen eye and thoughtful feedback helped me shape these words into their truest form. Your insights have been invaluable.

Lastly, to my readers. Thank you for opening your hearts to these poems. It is your willingness to connect, to feel, and to journey alongside me that makes this endeavour worthwhile.

With gratitude and love,
Yusra

1. I Found Peace

He did not love me as he promised,
He made a pool of lies
and left me drowned,
So, I gathered myself
took the deepest breath,
I have ever taken,
Let the wind guide me,
the sun glistening my body,
I stitched my wounds
with strings of gold,
while walking on the empty roads,
Shining and sparkling
in the moonlight
And I realised I don't
need anyone to embrace
me or put me at ease,
And in that moment,
I found peace.

2. Will I ever be able to heal?

Will I ever be able to heal?
To stitch the wounds that time cannot seal?
The echoes of pain, like ghosts in the night,
Haunt my heart, robbing it of light.

I've carried the weight, year after year,
A burden of sorrow, a river of fear.
Each step forward, the past pulls me back,
Tracing old scars on a well-worn track.

The world says time mends every tear,
But some nights, the ache is too much to bear.
I question the truth of that tired refrain—
Is healing just hope, or freedom from pain?

Yet, in the stillness, a whisper I hear,
A soft, steady voice, calm and sincere:
"You are not broken, though bruised you may feel.
Even the earth takes time to heal."

The stars, they remind me, they've seen it before—
The shattered, the lost, washed up on the shore.
And still, they shine, steadfast and whole,

A map of resilience etched in my soul.

Perhaps healing's not a finish line,
Not a perfect state, but a crooked design.
A mosaic of moments, a patchwork of care,
A journey of learning that I'm still here.

Will I ever be able to heal?
The answer is there, though the path may conceal.
Each day I rise, each breath I take—
Healing's a promise I'll slowly remake.

3. Celestial Muse

Beneath the stars, where silence sings,
I trace your name in cosmic rings.
The moon, a poet, begins to write,
Of you, its muse, in silver light.
The galaxies spin in a lover's dance,
Each twinkling star a stolen glance.
Nebulas bloom, their colors ignite,
A canvas of you in the endless night.
Comets streak like whispered desire,
Their fiery trails a burning choir.
The void, though vast, feels soft and near,
When your essence fills the atmosphere.
Each constellation's a story to take—
You are the theme of every love poem I make.

4. A Fragile Chance

She stood on a cliff of her own despair,
Eyes hollowed out by the weight she'd bear.
Each breath a shiver, each step a plea,
For love to stay, for someone to see.

She dared to dream through her haunted past,
A fragile hope she thought might last.
With trembling hands, she unlocked the door,
And let someone in, though her heart was sore.

She gave her all, every piece she could find,
Her laughter, her love, her broken mind.
She stitched herself into something whole,
And offered it up—her aching soul.

But then, like a whisper, they slipped away,
Leaving her crumbling, a castaway.
Her voice cracked open, a cry to the skies,
"Why am I left? Why do love's promises die?"

The echoes came back, empty and bare,
Mocking her faith, her desperate care.
She clawed at the ground, tears carving streams,

Drowning in sorrow, shredding her dreams.

"Was I unworthy? Did I try too much?
Did my love suffocate with its tender touch?
Why do I keep breaking, again and again?
What's left of me after this endless pain?"

But hear this truth, though her heart may bleed,
Her love was a gift, not a desperate need.
It shone too bright for fleeting eyes,
A diamond unseen beneath cloudy skies.

Her tears are rivers that will carve the stone,
Until she builds a kingdom of her own.
And though it hurts, so raw, so deep,
The seeds of her strength will quietly keep.

One day, her tears will water the earth,
And flowers will bloom to prove her worth.
And someone will come, steady and true,
To cherish the soul that no one knew.

But for now, it's okay to cry,
To grieve the hope that said goodbye.
For every tear she sheds tonight,
Is proof she loved with all her might.

5. Left In The Shadows

She dared to dream, after years of night,
A heart long hidden, she brought to light.
With cautious steps, she let him near,
A trembling soul wrapped in fragile fear.

For once, the world felt warm, alive,
A love she thought could help her thrive.
She poured her soul, her every hue,
Her deepest red, her softest blue.

But love, it seems, was a fleeting guest,
A storm that left her heart distressed.
One day he vanished, without a word,
Her cries unanswered, her voice unheard.

Abandoned, discarded, like she was none,
Her fragile hope came undone.
"Was I too much, or far too small?
Did I love too freely? Was I wrong to fall?"

She stares at mirrors, but hates the face,
The girl who trusted, now out of place.
Each moment aches, her chest feels tight,
Her heart a shadow, her soul a fight.

"I gave my all, my tender care,
But was it a burden too heavy to bear?
Am I broken, flawed, a love untrue?
Or is love itself a cruel, false view?"

Her hands grow numb, her heart turns cold,
The fear of loss takes its hold.
Each path ahead feels laced with dread,
A trap, a snare, a love misled.

And so, she sits in the quiet despair,
Clutching her heart that no one will repair.
Her hope now ashes, her love a scar,
A wound that whispers, "You've gone too far."

She longs to move, but cannot rise,
Her dreams lie buried beneath the skies.
For every piece of herself she gave,
Now rests alone in love's dark grave.

6. The Weight of Regret

I carry the weight of broken things,
The love I gave that never took wings,
To someone who never saw the cost,
Of all the trust and time I lost.

I regret the moments I didn't seize,
The chances that slipped, the paths I'd leave.
I wasn't at the right place, the right time,
Now all I have are the echoes of rhyme.

The silence of waiting, the fear of the fall,
The actions I didn't take, the ones I recall.
The roads not walked, the words unsaid,
The dreams left hanging, half-dead.

I regret not moving when the heart called,
The moments I hesitated, the times I stalled.
I regret the love that turned to dust,
The pieces of myself I didn't trust.

But regrets, they don't define who I am,
I am not the ashes, nor the broken plan.
For in the ruins, new roots grow deep,
And from the sorrow, I'll learn to leap.

I'll take the lessons, not the weight,
For the future's open, unsealed by fate.
And though regrets will come and go,
I will rise again, and let them flow.

Love will return, but with more care,
I'll be the right place, the right time, aware.
For I am still whole, despite the scars,
A soul that learns to reach for stars.

7. To Feel Love's Fire Again

She stands at the brink of a restless sky,
A heart that aches but dares to try.
The weight of heartbreak, the sting of past,
She longs for a love that will truly last.

To forget the tears, the sleepless nights,
The empty words and endless fights.
To erase the scars etched deep in her soul,
And feel again what once made her whole.

She craves the rush, the reckless glow,
The first love's dance she used to know.
The way her heart raced, her breath grew light,
A fire igniting the darkest night.

No bitter taste, no clenching pain,
No memories of love left in vain.
Just open fields, a boundless start,
An untouched, unguarded, unbroken heart.

She dreams of love so wild, so pure,
A balm, a spark, a radiant cure.
To feel alive, to let joy reign,

To taste love's fire and forget the pain.

Though time has carved its mark within,
She yearns to let the light begin.
For love, she knows, can heal, can mend—
She'll rise, she'll leap, she'll love again.

8.

Maybe, Just Maybe

What if someday, someone will come,
And all my fears will come undone
What if they stay, what if they care,
What if they see the pain I bear

What if someone reads my eyes,
And knows the truth behind my disguise
What if they see I'm broken inside,
And piece me together, side by side

What if they make me smile so bright,
And fill my days with warmth and light
What if they hold my hand for no reason,
And stay through every storm and season

What if they show me who I could be,
And love the parts no one can see
What if they stay, no matter what,
A love so deep, i won't forget.

What if someone is out there still,
Waiting to love me, and always will

What if my dreams aren't far away,
And love will find me, maybe one day.

8. The Depth of Nothing

What's going on in your mind, you ask.
A storm, a flood, a thousand untamed thoughts—
but my lips betray me,
and I say, "Nothing.
It's just nothing."

Why do I say that?
Because the truth feels too heavy to hold,
or maybe too light to matter.
Because finding the answer
means facing it,
and what if the answer is so simple
it splits me open?

Do people scare you, you ask?
Sometimes.
The way they see too much,
the way they look away.
But still, I say,
"Nothing."

What makes me scared, you ask.
Everything—
the shadows that stretch,

the silence that swells,
the weight of tomorrow.

But before I can speak,
you cut through me,
"I know—your answer is nothing".

But explain a little bit of that nothing to me."

And you're right.
But nothing isn't empty.
Nothing is the darkness I can't escape,
the quiet that screams too loud.
Nothing is what I fear the most.

So, with a smile, I say-
Nothing scares me.

9. A love In Disguise

She swore her heart was hers to keep,
Bound by silence, buried deep.
But then he came, all charm and grace,
A dream disguised, a fleeting face.

He whispered vows of endless skies,
Wrapped her soul in tender lies.
With every word, her guard gave way,
To find his love was made of clay.

She begged for crumbs, a fleeting glance,
For just a thread of true romance.
But silence answered, cold and stark,
And left her clinging in the dark.

Her chest grew heavy, breaths grew tight,
An anxious war through endless night.
Each memory turned sharp and raw,
What was her flaw? What did he saw?

She counted cracks within her soul,
Did her love demand too high a toll?
Or was she doomed to be cast aside,
A heart too soft for the stormy tide?

Yet even in the ruin's ache,
A truth began to gently wake.
Her love was rare, her heart too kind,
To let his shadows cloud her mind.

For none could dim the light she held,
The love that swelled and still rebelled.
One day, she knew, the pain would fade,
And love would come, unscarred, unplayed.

But for now, she wept, she bled, she grew,
A tender heart, both brave and true.
In every tear, her strength would rise,
A phoenix soaring through broken skies.

11. Before Everything Turned Blue

I wish I could tell you, before it all turned blue,
How much I adored the way you smiled—so true.
The stolen glances, though subtle and fleet,
I caught every one, a secret so sweet.

The little things you did, though you thought them small,
Were treasures to me, the grandest of all.
The first chocolate, the flowers you gave,
I've hidden them under my bed, to save.

The way you caressed the strands by my ear,
Your teasing words, your laugh sincere.
You made me blush, you lit up my sky,
Yet I kept my love locked, too scared to try.

The night you stood beneath my home,
Your surprise made the stars feel less alone.
I watched from my balcony, joy running wild,
In that fleeting moment, I felt love's child.

I feared if I gave too much of my heart,

You'd drift away, we'd break apart.
So I made you chase, kept you near,
Hoping that would hold you here.

But my fears, it seems, were always true,
For when I begged, I least mattered to you.
In my darkest hours, you turned away,
Left me grasping at hopes that began to fray.

Now I linger, caught in a tangled bind,
Between love remembered and peace of mind.
Do I desire you, or crave release?
My heart's in pieces, I long for peace.

I wish I could tell you, before it all turned blue,
But now it's too late—the story is through.

12. Kind of Love

What kind of love do you seek?
The kind that feels like home,
that settles deep in your chest,
steady, unshaken, true.

How do you know about these little things? you ask—
Because I know you, kind of love.
You are the first person I think of every morning,
kind of love.

The first person I run to when words spill out,
kind of love.

Hold me without a reason,
kind of love.

You rest, and I'll cook for you,
kind of love.

I brought your favorite flowers—
because they make you smile,
kind of love.

I'll wipe the tears you try to hide,

kind of love.

I can't let you leave without a kiss,
kind of love.

I'll stay awake, just to listen
to your heartbeat while you sleep,
kind of love.

This song reminded me of you—
every note wrapped in your presence,
kind of love.

I'll make you laugh
until the weight falls away,
kind of love.

Oh, to feel this—to be seen,
to be held in a way that feels infinite.

The kind of love that makes the world quiet,
and whispers softly:
You are enough.

13. The Chapters

Isn't it strange,
when a chapter feels too heavy,
and the ink spills into your soul,
you want to close the book
but the words hold you,
whispering, *"Stay."*

You cannot skip the sorrow,
for it is the mirror of your heart.
The wounds you wish to forget
are the ones that heal you,
if you let them.

Every character you meet
is a reflection of some part of you.
The ones who break you,
the ones who lift you,
they are all walking the same path.

Not every page brings peace.
Some pages burn,
others freeze,
but they are all leading you
to where the light is waiting,

just beyond the shadow.

You can close your eyes to the storm,
but the storm will still pass through you.

You cannot run from what's inside—
it is the very thing that will guide you
to your own soul's deep, quiet song.

So live it,
even when you tremble at the words,
even when the chapters seem endless,
for it is in the turning
that you will find yourself.

You are not lost.
You are unfolding.
Each chapter is a prayer,
and the world spins
on the thread of your becoming.

14. Beyond Words

The truth is this—
no matter how soft the words may be,
they can't comfort you the way
a presence can set you free.

Words may promise,
but they break with time,
it's the steady touch
that feels truly sublime.

You can whisper love,
but can you hold it near?
It's in the actions,
the proof that's clear.

In the end,
it's not what's spoken or heard,
but the way you show it—
actions speak louder than words.

15. Unspoken

She sits on her bed,
alone in the stillness of night,
hands clenched to her knees,
fingers tight with the fight.

"Please," she whispers,
her voice trembling low,
"I still love him,
but I don't want to love him anymore."

Tears fall like rain,
but her heart is a storm,
torn between holding on
and wanting to be reborn.

"Please help me forget,"
she pleads to the empty air,
"Help me let him go,
I can't keep living in despair."

Her face is a map of pain,
each tear a silent cry,
lost between wanting release
and the love she can't deny.

"Please, I don't want to hurt,"
the words barely form,
but she knows deep inside,
this love is what keeps her warm.

Yet warmth feels like fire,
and fire burns too bright—
she clutches her knees tighter,
fighting the dark of the night.

"Please help me forget,"
she whispers once more,
as the tears keep falling,
her heart begging for the door.

4o mini

16. Fragile Hearts

In the quiet of their restless mind,
Thoughts twist like knots that never break,
They search for meaning in every sign,
Each word, each glance, a fear to take,
Haunted by the past they can't forsake.

They question everything, even love,
Worrying they've said too much or too little,
Each emotion feels too big to prove,
Yet with every heartbeat, they are brittle,
Fearing love will burn out like a candle's flicker.

The shadows come, and doubt fills the air,
What if the silence means they're gone?
A heart that bleeds, yet loves so rare,
Fearing abandonment all along,
Still, they cling to what feels like home.

They have loved deeply, but they've been torn,
The echoes of past pain never fade,
Afraid to let go, yet they're worn,
Haunted by memories that invade,
Still, they love with a heart that's afraid.

17. The Echo of Who I Was

The person I was is lost to the fire,
Her laughter consumed, her dreams undone.
She burned in the flames of grief and desire,
Her battle fought, yet her war never won.

She was reckless, wild, and full of flaws,
Ruled by a heart that bled too free.
Her hands would tremble, her spirit would pause,
But she still gave all that she could be.

From ashes she whispered, "Rise and transform,"
A voice that cracked beneath the strain.
I stood in the wreckage, weary and worn,
And learned to build from the ruins of pain.

The person I've become is stronger, it's true,
But the cost of her loss still leaves its trace.
Though time has healed and life feels new,
If you look deep enough into my eyes, you can still see
her weeping face.

18. Stormborne

Do not run from the storm in your chest.
It is not here to break you,
but to teach you how to dance with thunder,
how to sing beneath the weight of rain.

Your fear is a shadow,
cast by a fire that still burns within you.
Turn and face it—
see how it shrinks when you stand in its light.

Heartbreak may crack you open,
but oh, the beauty of a broken vessel!
It spills the soul like wine,
letting the world taste the sweetness you forgot was
there.

Anxiety claws at your throat,
whispering lies of your fragility.
Yet listen closely,
beneath its noise, there is a voice saying,
"Breathe, beloved. You are still here."

Strength is not a fortress of stone;
it is the root that clings to the earth

even when the wind howls its fiercest song.
It is the seed buried deep in the cold,
trusting spring will come again.

Rise now, like the sun after long nights.
You have carried this weight
because you were meant to grow strong.

The wound may remain,
but it has made you vast,
a sky wide enough to hold the stars.

Do not fear your journey,
for every step forward
is the answer to the fear behind you.

You are not broken.
You are becoming.

19. Fifty Years, Forever, and Beyond

How do I find a love that lasts fifty years and long?
I smiled and said,
Fifty years is long, yes—so very long,
But to reach forever,
You must first cross a thousand bridges within.

Resilience will be your lantern,
Patience your compass.
You will stumble through storms of disagreement,
Face battles born of silence and sharp words.
But more than anything,
You must master the art of forgiveness.

To stay with one soul,
To see them, truly see them—
Not as perfect, but as whole,
Flawed and divine in their brokenness—
That is when fifty years will feel like a fleeting blink.
And in that moment,
You will hunger for forever.

Oh, there will be days of trembling.
Fear will clutch your chest,

The fear of losing the one whose presence
Feels like your very breath.
And when you feel it—
Look.
Look into their eyes.
Watch how your anger softens,
How love—a quiet, unbreakable thread—remains.

Oh, you will not make it without pain,
For love blinds and binds,
And in blindness,
Words of unkindness may slip.
But love, like a patient sculptor, shape your souls,
Even through the cracks and bruises.

Love is beautiful, yes,
But it is harder to love than to hate.
So take this wisdom,
This greater advice:

Learn to forgive, my friend.
Learn to let go of the small and the sharp.
Learn to trade your fleeting grudges
For fifty years of love,
And perhaps,
For a forever that reaches beyond the stars.

20. A Home in You

I yearn for a home,
Not just walls and a roof,
But a sanctuary where sunsets feel like whispered prayers—
Dreamy, eternal.
A little porch to sit,
With a coffee table that gathers stories
And a vase of flowers to hold the day's tenderness.

I dream of a kitchen,
Where the walls echo with laughter,
And every step is laced with the nostalgic aroma
Of mornings that taste like forever.
A window where birds perch like poets,
And clouds drift as if spun from dreams.

There must be a small library,
With shelves wrapped in warm light,
And a fireplace murmuring,
"Movies, chill, and love."
But most of all,
This home needs you.
The breakfast table is bare
Without the flowers you bring,

Plucked from the garden of your affection.

The kitchen feels hollow
Without the coffee you brew,
Each cup steeped in your care.
The library waits patiently,
For your warmth to grace its corner,
For your voice to read the words aloud—
Every syllable a gift.

The porch begs for a swing,
Where I can watch the sun dip below the horizon,
Held safe in your arms,
While the fireplace—
Ah, the fireplace—
Is merely a shadow without your kisses
To light its flame.

I yearn not for walls,
But for the soul within them.
I yearn for you.

You are the home I seek,
The hearth that warms me,
The porch where my heart rests,
The place where every dream takes root.
I yearn for a home in you.

21. My Favourite Unfinished Story

I wish I could see you again,
The best surprise my heart ever knew—
A serendipity I thought lived only in stories,
Yet you stood there,
A chapter I never thought to write.

I asked the stars,
"Why do souls meet,
If they are not meant to stay?"
But their only answer
Was the echo of what we once were.

I built castles in the air,
Dreams with open doors waiting for your footsteps,
But you never came.

Now, I miss you every day—
I read your words,
Play the songs that carry your name,
And I fear the silence between us
Will erase what the universe once wove together.

Though we cannot be,

I must tell you:
You are my favourite in another multiverse,
The "what if" that lingers in my soul,
The almost that aches like an unfinished melody,
The story I still read,
Even though the ending is lost.

You are my favourite unfinished story.
And in every realm where love exists,
I hope we find each other again.